ABUNDANCE

FOR THE TIMES YOU FEEL A LITTLE TOO MUCH

HARSHI UPADHYAY

Made with ♥ on the Notion Press Platform
www.notionpress.com

Contents

Contents

Acknowledgements

I would like to express my deepest gratitude to my mentor, Ma'am Susan Mark, for the profound impact you've had on my literary path. Your passion for literature ignited my love for words.

To my teacher, Sajana Morris Ma'am, thank you for always pushing me to be my best and helping me grow as a writer. Your encouragement has made all the difference.

A shoutout to my sister, Shruti, for patiently listening to me rant about this book for hours on end—you've been my greatest sounding board.

Lastly, my heartfelt appreciation goes to my friend, Tarang, for the beautiful illustrations and the meticulous editing that brought this project to life.

Prologue

In this anthology, we explore the timeless journey of love through its three most defining stages: **TheLoving, The Hurting, and The Healing**.

In **TheLoving**, we delve into the magic of connection, where hope and passion bloom effortlessly, painting a picture of the beginning—filled with warmth, joy, and the promise of forever.

But as the pages turn, we encounter **TheHurting**, a stage where that same love is tested. Betrayal, loss, and pain surface, stripping away the rosy hues and forcing us to confront the fragility of the heart.

Yet, through these moments of despair, we arrive at the final stage: **The Healing**. Here, we witness the resilience of the soul as it learns to mend, rediscovering strength, self-love, and the possibility of beginning again.

Set in varied times and places, each piece reflects the universal rhythm of human emotions, mirroring the ways in which love transforms us, breaks us, and ultimately, heals us. This anthology invites readers to experience the raw, beautiful cycle of love—an ever-evolving force that shapes who we are.

THE LOVING

'And in that moment, I swear we were infinite.'

Perks of being a wallflower

1. MILES OF ME

when we meet again and you lean in
to breathe life into my dull blue lips
to taste longing on my tongue
and sense the pulse on my neck
don't you stop there
I've got miles of skin
skin left unmarked , unkissed
envious of my now warm lips
there's pulse on my neck but also on my breast
my lips aren't as dull as the color of my waist my back
they are so eager
to feel how my tongue felt being savored
my arms get a reasonable share of you, but
what about my thighs, I promised
they won't go unnoticed, this time
I promised my belly it won't ache
because you'll kiss the butterflies
and they'll stop going crazy, my shoulder blades
are starting to complain
you haven't so much so carved a single letter of your name
my earlobe rings and begs your moans
my hips now sore from your firm hold
they need soothing too

just like my back aching a caress
it's sad that you only know about the mole on my nape
and not the one three inches below my waist
and look you stopped
what made you
how could you
stop, when I gave you all of me
miles of me
and you seem content with only a few centimeters.

2. 2:59 AM

3:00 AM
Empty streets
Wandering alone
With my toxic heart
Is a nightmare.

3:00 AM
Empty streets
Wandering alone
With you
Is a day dream.

3. RAVENOUS EYES

"what is it with your obsession with eyes?

to begin with
they tell me more about you
than your lips ever do
they tell me that you lie
when you say you don't care
but they light up every time I walk by
they tell me that you're scared
to let feelings take over
let the eyes talk for once
say your truth being sober
don't let the brows arch a question mark
trust your gut
and watch life take over.

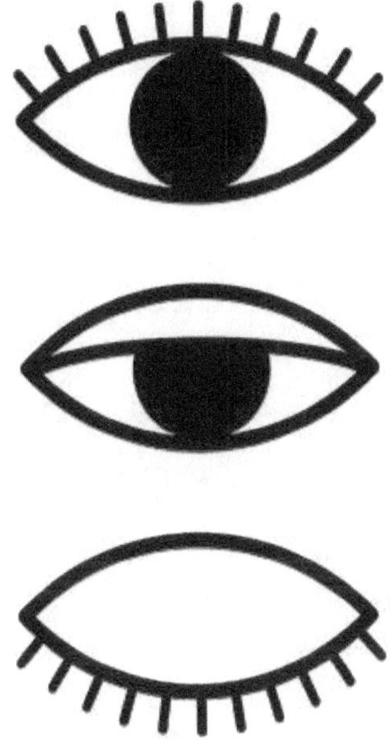

4. TRIP TO BLISS ROAD

The day I met you
The clouds of confusion started to disappear
My heart spoke loud and clear
But the words couldn't reach my mouth
They didn't need to
For my body spoke it all
When I savoured the taste of your tongue
As my hands stuck to the nape of your neck
While yours wandered through my waist
No better way than this to convey my message
My body perfectly spoke your language.

5. NEURONS

it has come to a point where
my brain refuses to think
if the thoughts aren't of you.

6. STILL AND HUSHED

you were red in the white -of the crowd
you were hushed in the noise -of the crowd
you were still in the stream -of the crowd
you were true in the lie of the crowd
maybe that is what attracted me
that you saw what no one could see
but I saw you
wondering what a red in the white would do?
will it make the white pink?
or let the majority win.
will the truth ever be heard?
or was it its own choice
to stay still and hushed.

7. CRYPTIC

oh how when I open my eyes,
I see him
when my hands travel down my thighs
somewhat naturally, my mind
shifts to his
neck
shoulders
arms
fingers
and I'm left wondering why.

8. SUMMER BREEZE

"Do you think I am pretty?" I asked
"like the sun setting on a deep blue sea
but also the dawn and the light pink hue
like that first sip of your morning tea
and like how I always knew,
that someday when you ask me
whether I think you're pretty
how I could never just say yes or no
because 'pretty' isn't enough
for your kind of beauty it's too weak, too low
if pretty can sum up
that one breeze of chilly air midst hot summer
and warm hugs in winter cold
or cuddles from my lover
if pretty is as whole as the universe
and as essential as the atom
if in pretty all gods immerse
and if pretty is what a simpleton cannot fathom
then yes,
yes you are,
yes you are pretty." he answered.

THE HURTING

'*These violent delights*
have violent endings
and in their triumph die
like fire and powder
which as they kiss consume'

William Shakespeare
Romeo and Juliet

9. ROCK BOTTOM

it took me a while
but eventually I realized where I went wrong
falling in love wasn't a mistake
but loving with my heart and not my eyes was
falling in love wasn't a mistake
but loving the person and not their scandalous skin was
falling in love wasn't wrong
but mistaking their sensuality for passion was
falling in love wasn't a mistake
but loving the wrong person the right way was
falling in love?
it had to happen.
they made it so obvious
falling in love wasn't a mistake
but wanting them to love me too was.

10. MIRROR AND I

every time you tell me I look beautiful
I feel beautiful
and the times you forget
are the times I stand in front of the mirror
staring in regret
I try to convince myself
'red is not my color'
'maybe it's the dress'
I stand for hours
searching for ways to impress
you
so you'd maybe take notice of me
and kiss me on the cheek
say I look pretty
now that I've run out of shades
and tried every last ivory dress
as your memory of me fades
I'm convinced
it wasn't the dress
and *I haven't felt pretty since...*

11. PARASITE

is it really that normal
is it really that easy
to see eye as strangers
3 days after you kissed me
oh so passionate
because you held me so tight
oh so deep
did that not suffice?
I should've seen that coming
Afterall
you were *nothing but a parasite.*

12. LIGHTNING

how could the darkness possibly have drowned me
when my man had the speed of light
I hope whoever kept him busy that night
was worth the sacrifice
that our love was.

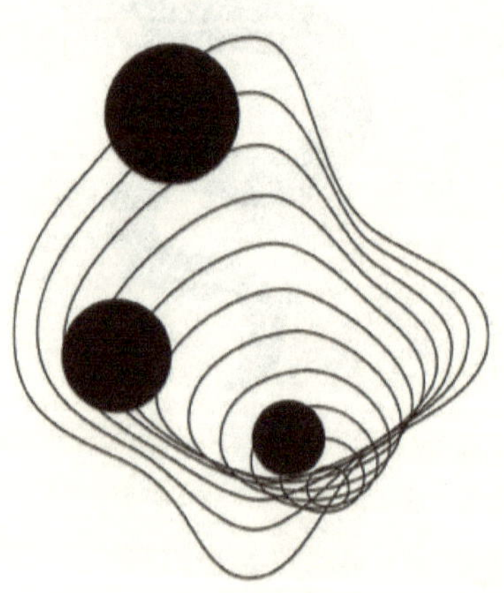

13. SILENT QUESTIONS

it's been three days, four

a week, now two

all the glances in the corridor

still nothing from you,

I know the silence in itself is an answer

but it's my hopeless romantic heart

that will just keep waiting

for you.

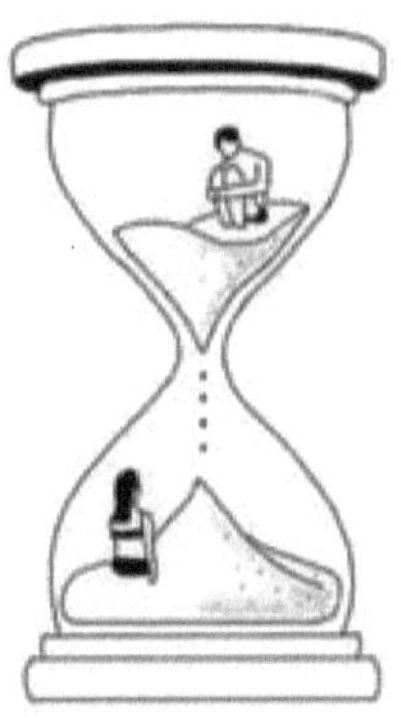

14. YOUNG AND DUMB

I was in love

and he was the one

the one who had me question my life choices

I was in love

so naive and young

part of the reason now love feels so hopeless

I was in love

when he wanted fun

wait till I tell you the fun he was hoping

I was in love

and they say love is blind

so, I gave in the time he spread me on the bedsheet

eyes closed

fingers clutched

the white of the sheet now red beneath me

he'll finally be mine

I gave him what he wanted right?

next morning when I picked up the phone

to tell him I couldn't feel my legs, thighs, face

nor my soul

the caller tune went straight to voice note.

15. KEY TO YOUR OWN COFFIN

I know you dreamed of
a poetic life
with him beside
for things to work out
and him to stay
you to find an ending
to this agony ascending

so you gave him your key
and called him your home
hoping he'd release your hurting soul
but he buried the key
took out nails instead
and with the hammer that his heart was
dug yours inside a coffin bed.

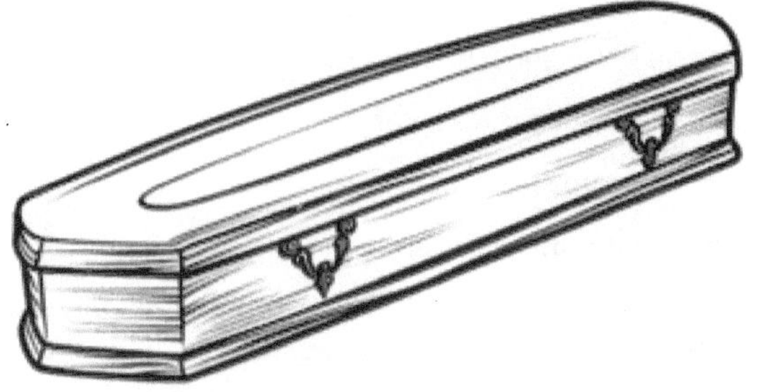

16. MINT CHAPSTICK

I know your eyes still search for me
in a room full of strangers
and that you gaze my crimson cheek
and lips, reminiscing the flavor
of my strawberry mint Chapstick
you used to religiously savour
along with my vanilla neck
where you'd leave your initials
and today when I glance back
we go back to being strangers
like how we once used to.

17. ACROPHOBIA

why would you?
how could you?
take me to dinner dates
hold the door on our way out
get me flowers
my favorite kind
had me feeling so high
higher than I can digest
higher than I can survive
only to kiss my cheek
the final goodbye

what do I do with our future I planned
and what do I do with this *new found fear of heights.*

THE HEALING

*'I'm out with lanterns
looking for myself'*

Emily Dickinson

18. DROUGHT

I've come to realize that
it doesn't matter how it ended
what matters is that it did,
for my heart could no longer endure
the torture that loving you was
because all it did was pour
and pour
and pour
till all there left was
a drought

it's time to love me an ocean.

19. CHOOSING TO NOT FIT IN

it is when the chatterbox in me became silent
when my own opinions became irrational
when my coping mechanisms became violent
and I no longer spoke with passion of my aspirations
I knew I had to leave.

20. CITY LIGHTS

I used to be a simple girl
the city has surely changed me
because the pain of burning in agony
has overpowered the grief of burning in the first place at all
I no more wear contentment up my sleeves
and lost my grace somewhere in the fall
but I refuse to be
like the people around
who are blinded by city lights
and deafened by rush hour sounds

I demand my simplicity
I demand my peace.

• 45 •

21. MOONLIT CONVERSATIONS

There's a huge difference between
having a heart that's healed
and a heart that's kept on hold,
its healed you say?
then why do you fear the nights?
it's easy to keep yourself occupied when the sun rise
but the reasons to not let your mind fumble upon those words
time and time again during the night are hard to find.
I understand
I understand why you've been avoiding conversations with the
moonlit nights.

22. R.I.P.

Now that it's all over
All the time I spent with him will feel a waste
But I'll waste some more
Thinking about that fine poetic face.
I will cry till I have no tears left
But not once will I compare myself
To the girls or the one he made feel
The same as I
Nor shall any doubt themselves
By the end of the 3rd verse, he was already dead
In my mind
May his soul rest in peace.

23. PAPER BOATS

oh how did we go
from reading bed time stories
to overthinking in the dark

from making paper boats
to sailing oceans apart

from crying loud
and laughter so emphatic
to sobbing in a pillow
avoiding being dramatic

talking all night long bout our passions
to me writing this poem
and you nodding yeses.

24. VAGABOND

somebody told me moving on was easy
that somebody was thoroughly wrong
because here I am leaving the city
in an attempt to move on
but the way I pack your memories
in a discrete compartment
I'm worried will leave me
travelling city to city
country to country
to a whole new continent.

25. 02/04/2024

02/04/2024
I woke up a little early
went out for a walk
had my everyday coffee
that tasted nothing like every day
I laughed a little louder
smiled a little brighter
bought flowers for myself
I'm finally making a home out of the asylum you left.

26. SCALES

if my true colors drive people away
then I am better off alone.

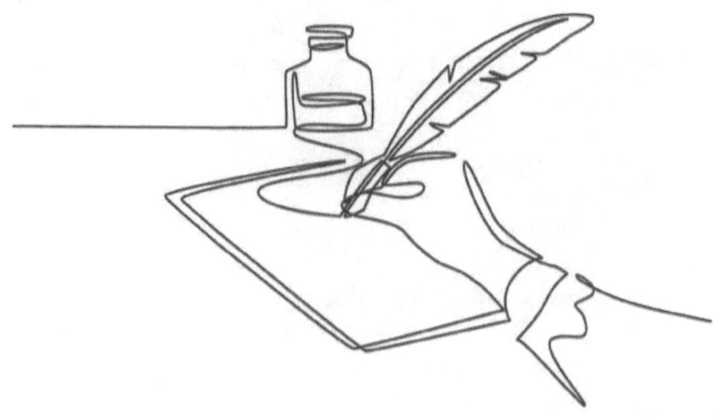